Stress Management

Thorsons First Directions

Stress Management

Vera Peiffer

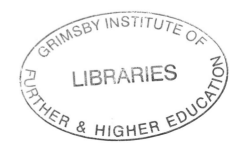

Thorsons
An Imprint of HarperCollins Publishers
77–85 Fulham Palace Road,
Hammersmith, London W6 8JB

The Thorsons website address is:
www.thorsons.com

Published by Thorsons 2001

10 9 8 7 6 5 4 3 2 1

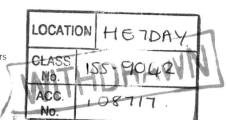
Text derived from *Principles of Stress Management*, published by Thorsons 1996

Editor: Jo Kyle
Design: Wheelhouse Creative
Production: Melanie Vandevelde
Photographs from PhotoDisc Europe

A catalogue record for this book is available from the British Library.

ISBN 0 00711034 0

Printed and bound in Hong Kong

Always consult your doctor for any serious or long-term health problem.
The information in this book is not intended to be taken as a replacement for medical advice.

Contents

Stress Management

is dealing with stress in a positive way to ensure

good health and general well-being

What Stress Is

Anyone who has ever had to struggle through a prolonged period of work overload, be it at home or in the workplace, will know what it feels like to be physically exhausted and mentally overwrought. Whereas you are perfectly capable of dealing competently with life's ups and downs when you are unstressed, any hiccups in the daily routine become an emotional crisis once the pressure exceeds a certain threshold.

Stress and its unpleasant side-effects can arise from a great many different factors; work overload is just one of them. Other life events which can put you under pressure are changes in your circumstances, for example if a family member gets seriously ill or you unexpectedly suffer financial difficulties. As a rule of thumb you could say that any event that significantly changes your daily routine is a potential trigger for stress. I say 'potential' because a lot will depend on your general attitude to change. Stress is not just generated by circumstances; your attitude towards the circumstances will have a significant impact on how you cope: A small amount of stress is useful; it adds interest and motivation to life and keeps us on our toes. Changes that we perceive

as moderate are not just harmless but also invigorating, as our adaptability needs to be trained regularly to stay in working order. As we practise going with the flow and dealing with changes, we become stronger. However, when the changes become too great or when they influence our lives negatively over a period of time, our capacity to adapt can become overstretched and it can make us ill.

In extreme cases, prolonged exposure to stress can lead to physical and/or emotional breakdown.

Defining stress

You will already have noticed that stress is not a clear-cut matter which can be defined in objective terms. You may find that the best way of describing stress is at a totally subjective level, as any change that makes you feel uncomfortable physically or emotionally. This definition allows for individual differences in attitude and perception towards stressors.

A subjective definition also makes it clear that stress is not the same thing as a great workload, a lot of responsibility or having demands made on you. If these scenarios were automatically synonymous with

stress, then *nobody* could be expected to experience them free of stress. However, there are people who have a lot to do and yet stay unstressed by it; there are people who carry great responsibility and who cope with it very well. Stress is only partly a result of the situation itself; it is also, to an extent, caused by our attitude towards that situation. This explains why different people react differently to stress.

Physical stress responses

Physiologically, the same thing happens to all of us when stress sets in. As soon as we perceive a situation as potentially threatening, our primitive stress response of 'fight or flight' springs into action. Our breathing rate increases (thereby providing the brain and the muscles with more oxygen), the heart rate increases, blood-pressure rises, sugars and fats are released into the bloodstream for extra energy, muscles tense up, the flow of saliva decreases and perspiration increases. All our senses are on 'red alert', and adrenalin and cortisol are released which mobilize the body.

These spontaneous physical reactions are very useful when your house in on fire because they enable you to run faster and get away from danger more quickly. However, when you have the same automatic reactions when you are only thinking about tomorrow's meeting at work, you are in trouble. Whereas in the first instance all that extra physical energy and tension are put to good use, in the second example this excess energy has nowhere to go – as you sit there worrying about the next day's meeting, your stress hormones go round and round in your system, keeping everything buzzing in overdrive. For some people this

means an increase in gastric juice secretion, which can contribute to ulcers if the stress response kicks in on a regular basis. Also, the prolonged presence of stress and heavy demands on our ability to adapt can exhaust the body and increase the risk of damaging the function of organs such as the heart or the kidneys.

If you feel that you are particularly prone to unnecessary stress reactions, the following chapter should help you pinpoint the reasons for this.

Summary

- Stress can arise from many different factors.
- Small amounts of stress are necessary and beneficial.
- Certain personality types are more prone to stress than others.
- Prolonged stress can lead to illness or mental breakdown.
- The body reacts to stress by mobilizing physical responses to help us cope better with situations which we perceive as threatening.
- Even our thoughts can create a physical stress response.

Are You a Stress-prone Type?

We perceive changes and stressors in our own unique ways. Depending on our background, upbringing and present circumstances, we may find ourselves coping with stress much better than our neighbour or colleague at work. Some of us are born with greater resilience than others, enabling us to stay calm longer than the next person when the going gets tough.

Apart from resilience and adaptability to change, we also bring with us particular dispositions when we are born. Anyone who has children will be able to confirm how different they are right from the start. For example, one baby is placid and sleeps through the night very early on, whereas another baby will be more wakeful and excitable. These individual predispositions, together with the manner in which parents bring up their children, will result in various personality types – some of which are particularly vulnerable to stress.

The anxious type

This personality type will be lacking somewhat in self-confidence, unsure of his or her abilities even if others try to be reassuring. Anxious people are reluctant to express any negative emotions openly and are often incapable of saying 'no' if someone makes unreasonable demands on them. Even though anxious people appear to be conformist, they often harbour strong resentments against those whose wishes they seem to carry out so willingly.

Stress problems

Anxious people tend to go for undemanding jobs, which can easily lead them to becoming frustrated and bored. If they progress to a more responsible job they tend to feel easily hassled when the workload increases and will often take their unease out on others.

The perfectionist

Perfectionists like everything to be in its proper place and done at the proper time. Routine is of great importance, as is detail. Mistakes are not tolerated – they will even rewrite a handwritten, informal message if their pen slips or a word has been misspelled. This rather plodding way of dealing with life works out well as long as the job in hand is stable and predictable.

Perfectionists are usually hard-working and reliable, but not equipped to deal with sudden emergencies or change.

Stress problems

Their difficulties in adapting to change, and their unwillingness to give up established routines, can cause stress for perfectionists if they find themselves distracted from their routines. Their diligent attention to detail means that they are creating stress for themselves when better prioritization and a more relaxed approach to less important tasks could easily save the day.

The stimulus-seeker

This personality type thrives on risk and is often addicted to the rush of adrenalin which accompanies any venture. However, stimulus-seekers have a very limited attention span. They are often not concerned with detail and leave others to do the menial parts of a job while they attend to the 'big picture'.

Stimulus-seekers will typically choose professions where risk-taking promises to yield great amounts of money and/or esteem.

Stress problems

Stimulus-seekers experience the risks of their ventures as beneficial stress, and thrive on it. Their minds race with possibilities rather than worries, and as a consequence they tend to smoke and drink too much. Substance abuse and its negative side-effects are more common in stimulus-seekers than are mental and/or physical illness.

The ambitious type

Ambitious personalities tend to be hard-driven and aggressive, channelling all their energies into their work. They have problems delegating and are highly critical of themselves and others. They find it impossible to sit down quietly and do nothing – in times of stress they tend to do several things at the same time. They also find it hard to concentrate fully on conversations because they are already racing ahead in their mind, thinking about the next thing they want to do.

Stress problems

In their efforts to control everything and everyone around them, ambitious types exert themselves physically and mentally. They are unable to recognize when they have reached their limit and will typically suffer from high blood-pressure. They are prone to coronary heart disease, ulcers and atherosclerosis (hardening of the arteries).

All stress-prone types of personality are driven by one thing: fear. The anxious person is afraid to be unpopular and to be considered unhelpful; the perfectionist is afraid of being 'only human'; the stimulus-seeker is afraid of boredom; and the ambitious type is afraid of not being seen to achieve. Even though certain personality traits can predispose a person to have these fears, one's upbringing also plays a part. Below we look at some of the factors that can lead to a personality type that is vulnerable to stress.

Pressure to succeed

When children are pressurized by parents and teachers constantly to achieve the very best results, and if love and approval are dependent on high performance, some children will internalize these conditions and later live their lives accordingly. Self-worth becomes totally dependent on achievements.

Criticism

When criticized frequently and in an unconstructive manner, some children will withdraw, hoping to avoid further humiliation by keeping a low profile. They stop trying out new things, become anxious and unconfident in their own abilities and grow up to live their lives trying to please others and gain their approval in an attempt to maintain their own self-esteem.

Loneliness

When children are shown little or no affection or interest they can grow up without self-worth or confidence in their own validity as human beings. As a consequence, their entry into the adult world of work can constitute an escape from these feelings of worthlessness. In their attempt to justify their existence, they may dedicate themselves over-zealously to their work.

Overprotection

Parents who do everything for their children prevent them from becoming independent. This restrictive upbringing can lead to resentment and rebellion, coupled with great fear at what there is 'out there'. As overprotected children grow up they keep on struggling with the same issues – not wanting to be controlled but at the same time fearing the freedom of being an independent person.

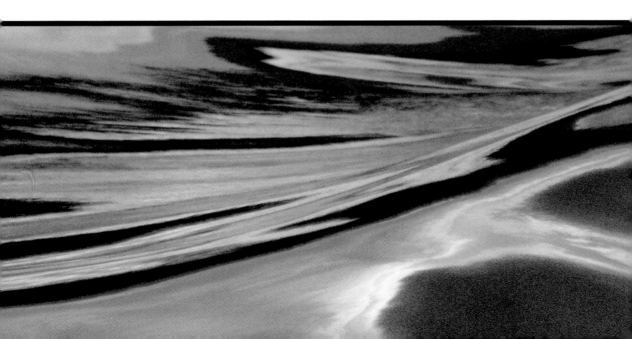

What is Causing You Stress?

As I have already mentioned, there are many different causes of stress, and what is stressful to one person will not be to another. While it is beyond the scope of this book to describe *all* the possible causes of stress, this chapter outlines some of the most common culprits.

Work stressors

The work environment is a veritable breeding ground for stress, for a variety of reasons. Wherever several people get together on a regular basis, tension becomes a possibility. Personalities can clash and rivalries often develop which lead to wranglings that have nothing to do with the job in hand.

Time pressure and deadlines are often part of a job and can cause a lot of stress. Deadlines are sometimes set by people not directly involved in a project, which means they may be unreasonably tight, or even impossible to meet. Unless you work for yourself, most people have to report to someone in a higher position, and a lot of stress can arise if the boss is not a good leader or communicator. And then there are the difficult colleagues ... Anyone who has ever worked with or for a difficult person will know how exhausting it can be.

Stress can also evolve directly from the working environment, for example, if you have to work with inadequate equipment. Physical stressors can also include bad lighting, poor ventilation, and pollutants (such as cigarette smoke) in the air.

Then there is the situation of working on your own. If there is no one to discuss job-related matters with you can easily end up lonely and isolated.

Domestic stressors

An obvious cause of stress at home is disagreement or tension among family members. This often arises from a basic incompatibility between partners – a particularly stressful problem as it tends to affect the whole family.

Children are another common cause of stress. Bringing up any child is difficult enough. However, if you have a child who is disabled or ill, that stress is compounded. Special children need a lot of help and attention, and loving parents will often end up exhausting themselves in the process. Of course, actual crises such as your child or anyone close to you dying is the most tragic life situation you can be faced with.

But it is not just one's immediate family that can cause stress. When elderly parents become too frail or unwell to look after themselves this can place tremendous stress on all the family, especially if one or both grandparents move into the family home. Certain stages in the life cycle, such as retirement, are also a time of stress, particularly when the family member has difficulty adapting to the change they are undergoing.

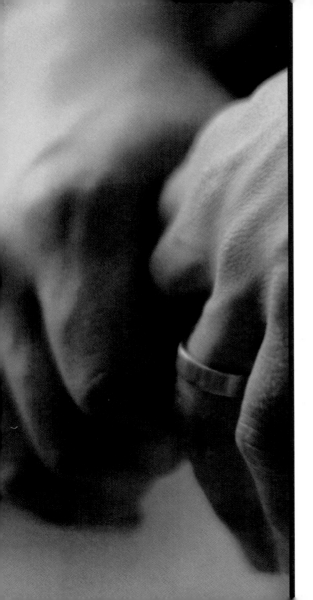

Other stressors

Any changes that disrupt your daily routine are stressful to a greater or lesser extent, depending on your general disposition and circumstances. When you lose your job, for example, this can cause a great deal of worry.

Interestingly, even what we consider to be *positive* changes can create stress, such as holidays or a promotion. When you are taken out of your familiar home or work environment, you will automatically have to adjust to your new situation, and this involves the expenditure of extra mental energy, often coupled with a sense of anxiety. Your immediate environment also has a great influence on your well-being.

If you live in an isolated area (whether in a rural backwater or an anonymous block of flats), stress can be brought about by the fact you have too little personal contact with people. Also, in areas where crime or violence are common, just leaving the house can be very stressful. Equally distressing are anti-social neighbours who play their music at top volume in the middle of the night, just as any other form of noise pollution (say from nearby airports or factories) can disturb your sense of equilibrium and, therefore, invoke a stress reaction.

What Happens When You Fall Into the Stress Trap...

It is important to understand the warning signals that your body and mind send out in response to a physical and emotional overload. By acquainting yourself with these stress symptoms you will be able to recognize and deal with them quickly and effectively, before they get out of hand.

There are some warning signs that people readily associate with stress, such as excessive smoking, tiredness, headaches and irritability. But did you know that the habit of checking and re-checking whether you have locked your front door or turned off the cooker is also a symptom caused by stress? Or were you aware that a bad memory can be a sign of stress?

Understanding which form stress can take also gives you a better choice of how to combat it. For example, you may decide that rather than popping a pill when a tension headache crops up you will learn to relax more fully (*page* 49).

Physical reactions

Our internal organs are controlled and regulated, without our conscious effort, by the autonomic (or vegetative) nervous system (ANS). The ANS consists of two antagonistic sets of nerves, the sympathetic and the parasympathetic nervous systems. The former connects the internal organs to the brain by spinal nerves; it prepares the organism for fight or flight when stress occurs. The nerve fibres of the parasympathetic nervous system, on the other hand, consist of cranial nerves and lumbar spinal nerves and have the task of getting the body back to normal after it has been aroused by the sympathetic nervous system.

This means that the sympathetic nervous system, once it is aroused, will set in motion a number of physical processes such as general muscle tension, dilation of the pupils, restriction of the flow of saliva in the mouth, dilation of the bronchi, opening of the pores and increased perspiration, constriction of the bowels and loosening of the bladder. In addition, the liver is activated to release sugar into the blood to produce extra energy, and hormones such as adrenalin and corticosteroids are pumped out into the system, accelerating breathing and increasing the heart rate. While all this is going on the autonomic nervous system slows down digestion processes. Once the stress-inducing situation is over, the parasympathetic branch of the nervous system reverses all the above processes – the pupils contract again, saliva starts flowing freely once more, the bronchi contract, the heart rate slows down, the pores close, the bladder contracts and digestion is stimulated, as is the release of bile which helps digest fats.

The Role of the mind

As you can see, physical symptoms are not all in the mind but are caused by very real changes in your blood chemistry, activated by the sympathetic nervous system. However, it is your mind that ultimately determines how strongly your body reacts to change or unusual circumstances. Depending on your attitudes, beliefs and general predisposition you will assess a situation as either harmless or dangerous. Some people positively thrive on challenges and are at their best when they need to deal with unforeseen situations; others will feel threatened and stressed.

Stress can be beneficial

The arousal of the sympathetic nervous system can be very beneficial, provided it does not come into play too often or too excessively. As I mentioned earlier, a slight increase in body tension, together with higher energy levels and the associated faster reaction time, is of great value if you have to perform well; it is when these reactions become excessive that problems result and we are less likely to cope well.

System overload

When the sympathetic nervous system is over-stimulated repeatedly and over a long period of time, your body may be able to adapt for a while, but as soon as any additional demands are made on it – such as those brought about by an unhealthy diet, smoking, drinking or lack of sleep – your system gets overloaded and can break down. Being in physical overdrive can become a habit, and if there is never a chance for the parasympathetic nervous system to kick into gear and reverse

the process, you wear down your inner organs.

Even though both the sympathetic and parasympathetic nervous systems are functioning on an involuntary level, we can activate the parasympathetic system by setting some time aside each day to relax properly – and this is not the same thing as putting up your feet and lighting a cigarette! Adapting your diet so that it contains more easily digestible foods also helps (*see page* 75), as does developing a more positive outlook (*see page* 68).

Warning signs of physical stress symptoms

- Tension (in the throat, chest, stomach, shoulders, neck, jaw)
- Headache and migraine
- Backache
- Neck ache
- Irregular breathing
- Palpitations
- Breathlessness even when at rest
- Restlessness and fidgeting
- Tics (face, eyes, mouth, etc.)
- Dry mouth
- High-pitched voice
- Sweating
- Cold hands and feet
- Shakiness
- Dizziness
- Exhaustion
- Stomach ache and 'butterflies' in stomach
- Indigestion
- Nausea
- Increased need to urinate
- Diarrhoea
- Sleeping problems
- Sexual problems
- Ulcers
- Increased sensitivity to noise

Mental and emotional reactions

The interdependence between body and mind, as described in the previous section, means that physical stress symptoms will affect your mental efficiency and emotional balance. Depending on how severely you experience stress, your mental and emotional symptoms will be more or less pronounced.

Mental symptoms

Typical mental reactions include racing thoughts and difficulty concentrating – as if your mind has gone into overdrive and is unable to slow down. This is why it is often impossible to go to sleep when you are stressed; your overactive mind will not let you! Apart from causing insomnia, this kind of muddled thinking and lack of concentration also leads to memory problems and difficulty retaining new information. Efficient recall depends on a focused and calm mind. If your mind is frantic no information will go into your memory and nothing can be retrieved from it, as anyone who has ever suffered from exam nerves will know.

The main effect of a stressed mind is that you lose your perspective. As your brain is racing ahead and you try in vain to keep up with it, you lose your balanced frame of reference. You have difficulties prioritizing sensibly, you feel unduly rushed – even when no one is rushing you – and you become disorganized. A certain symptom of stress is when you start lots of jobs but do not finish any of them.

Emotional symptoms

The emotional side-effects of stress are usually so unpleasant that the sufferer seeks relief after a while. Among the emotional responses are mood changes, aggression and tearfulness. Even if you are experiencing these emotional symptoms you may not be aware of them because they tend to progress gradually over time. We all have a certain capacity for adapting to stress and, as long as no further stress builds up on top of the original amount, we usually cope adequately – even though we might find ourselves a bit more short-tempered and cynical than before. These negative changes may not be apparent to us because we are too busy dealing with the issues that are making us feel stressed. It is when the stress will not abate that our impatience and cynicism start to grow, possibly out of proportion. Whereas we were reasonable and had a generally positive outlook before, we have now seemingly changed personality.

The way these emotional changes progress depends on your general predisposition. For example, some people become dejected, feel depressed and consider themselves a failure; others feel anxious or even panicky and struggle with feelings of guilt about their perceived inadequacy; still others develop phobias or tics or start suffering from nightmares.

Warning signs of mental stress symptoms

- Lack of concentration
- Forgetfulness
- Inability to remember recent events
- Inability to take in new information
- Lack of co-ordination
- Mind going around in circles
- Indecisiveness
- Irrational or rash decision-making

- Being disorganized
- Making mistakes more frequently
- Misjudging people and situations
- Inaccuracy
- Struggling with simple tasks (adding up, working simple machinery)
- Paying inordinate attention to detail

Warning signs of emotional stress symptoms

- Anxiety
- Phobias
- Panic attacks
- Feeling persecuted
- Aggression
- Cynicism
- Guilt
- Depression

- Mood swings
- Tearfulness
- Nightmares
- Feeling abandoned
- Excessive worrying
- Loss of sense
  of humour
- Withdrawal

Behavioural reactions

Some people, rather than displaying an overtly emotional reaction to stress, experience negative changes in their behaviour. Some of these changes in behaviour may not appear to be linked to stress at all. For example, when someone honks his horn and gesticulates wildly while we are sitting in a traffic jam we probably don't immediately think his problem is that he is over-stressed!

Our behaviour and reactions are governed by three factors – our personality, our past experiences, and our present circumstances.

Personality

Our personality will dictate our behavioural tendencies. If you are an introvert you are more likely to react to stress by withdrawing rather than by lashing out, as an extrovert might. A placid personality will have a much higher stress threshold than a 'racehorse' personality whose stress responses are triggered much earlier by more minor events.

Past experiences

Our past experiences will also contribute to our present-day behaviour. Past experiences, especially those in our childhood and adolescence, help form our attitudes and beliefs, and our expectations for the future. If, for

example, we have grown up in a loving and supportive environment where we received help when we had trouble dealing with a situation, we begin to learn how to deal with difficult situations without panicking. This means that we react much less readily to stress later on in life compared to those who have had guilt and shame heaped on them whenever they made a mistake or had problems learning something.

Present circumstances

Our present environment and circumstances also influence our behavioural reactions. I have already discussed the effects of environmental stressors like living in an unsafe neighbourhood or being subjected to noise pollution, for example. Equally, unexpected financial problems put enormous pressures on all of us. Even in these difficult circumstances a positive attitude and a constructive approach can be your saving grace. Happily, your attitude is something you can work on (*see page* 67) if you have not already developed a positive outlook in your younger years. Quite a few behavioural reactions to stress are an exaggeration of an existing habit. If you already have a slight tendency to overeat, bite your nails or worry, you will probably find that in times of stress you start bingeing, reducing your nails to half their size or developing obsessive thoughts or compulsive habits.

Obsessions and compulsions

The behavioural stress reactions that are hardest to understand are obsessions and compulsions. An obsession is a persistent idea or thought in your mind which terrifies you even though you know the thought is totally irrational. Obsessional thoughts come out of the blue and can be something like 'Today I am going to die' or 'Today I will harm my children.' Even though sufferers reject these thoughts, they are unable to stop them. In order to counteract these terrifying ideas the obsessive person will often go through a ritualistic compulsive action. This can be, for example, washing your hands every time you have touched anything, or checking continually that the ornaments on the mantelpiece are in a particular order. If anyone tries to stop this compulsive action, the sufferer gets extremely agitated and panicky.

A mild form of compulsion is one that many people go through as children – not stepping on cracks on the pavement. These mild forms are usually called superstitions and are fairly harmless. However, when a habit or thought begins to disrupt everyday life, the problem obviously needs professional attention.

People who develop obsessions and compulsions tend to be highly critical of themselves and others, have a strong perfectionist streak and are over-conscientious.

Warning signs of behavioural stress symptoms

- Increased smoking
- Increased drinking
- Overeating
- Eating only
  minimal amounts
- Eating nothing at all
- Neglecting personal
  appearance
- Driving aggressively
- Shutting yourself off
  from others
- Starting lots of things
  without finishing anything
  (chores at home, etc.)
- Nail-biting
- Hair-pulling
- Skin-picking
- Having obsessive
  thoughts and ideas
- Compulsive actions
  (checking and re-checking
  locks, lights, taps, etc.)

...And How to Climb Out of the Stress Trap

Having looked at the causes and symptoms of stress, we now come to some solutions. It is all well and good to understand the issues that are creating inner pressure for you and how this pressure manifests itself, but ultimately the crucial question is 'How can I get rid of the pressure?'

In this section you will find practical methods and techniques of combating stress. Clearly detailed exercises will help you get to grips with your particular problem area. Provided you practise the techniques regularly, you will soon get some relief from your stress symptoms. However, just *reading* about the techniques will not have any effect – some effort is required on your part!

So you thought you knew how to breathe...

We breathe day and night, 24 hours a day, whether we are aware of it or not. Although we can consciously control our breathing, it is generally an unconscious activity. Every time we breathe in, the ribs and muscles of the chest wall, as well as the diaphragm, help in the expansion and contraction of the lungs and distribute oxygen from the air into the bloodstream. Every time we breathe out, carbon dioxide is expelled from our lungs. The movements of breathing are regulated by several nerve centres in the brain. Cells in the brain stem are believed to control the rhythm and depth of breathing, while the vagus, or tenth cranial nerve, controls the blood vessels and bronchi of the lungs. Because the body stores practically no oxygen, any interference with breathing manifests immediately as a physical symptom such as dizziness, nausea or headaches, chest pains, shortness of breath or even fainting.

Even though the autonomic nervous system (our inner 'autopilot') keeps us breathing automatically without us having to attend to it consciously, our breathing is extremely susceptible to interference.

According to what mood we are in, how we are feeling and how these feelings change, our breathing will be fast or slow, regular or irregular, deep or shallow. And here we come to the relevance of breathing in the context of stress. As you experience any physical or emotional strain it will immediately affect your breathing, often in a detrimental way. At times of stress your breathing becomes irregular and shallow, with overlong periods during which you involuntarily hold your breath. This means that not enough oxygen gets to the brain, and this ultimately leads to an inability to concentrate, dizziness and a general feeling of agitation.

When you are affected by stress, correct breathing enables your body to relax and regain its natural equilibrium, at the same time calming your mind and making you feel in control again so that the anxiety (and its related symptoms) can abate. Before we look at a few exercises that will enable you to influence your breathing positively, I would like you to test whether you breathe correctly.

Test

- Lie down on your back, either on your bed or on the floor. Rest your head on a small pillow or a rolled up towel to give it support.
- Loosen any belt or tight waistband you may be wearing. Place one hand on your chest and the other hand on your belly area.
- Spend a few minutes lying still while you listen to a radio programme to distract yourself from your breathing.
- Once your body has settled down, begin to focus your attention on your hands and begin to observe which of your hands is being pushed up regularly by your in-breaths.

If only the hand on your *chest* is moving up and down, this means that your diaphragm stays stiff as you breathe and is therefore only permitting the top part of your lungs to be filled with air. This means that a great deal less oxygen is available to go to your internal organs, including your brain, than there would be if the lungs were fully inflated. At the same time not enough carbon dioxide is being expelled from your body, which negatively influences metabolism. Also, the lack of movement in the diaphragm means that both your liver and heart are insufficiently stimulated because the 'massaging' effect of diaphragmatic movement is absent. This results in insufficient circulation in your liver and heart.

If only the hand on your *belly* is moving up and down, this means that the top half of your lungs are not sufficiently 'aired' because most of the oxygen is going down into the bottom part of your lungs. Generally, breathing mainly through your belly area is better than breathing through your chest only, simply because the diaphragm is more mobile. The disadvantage, however, is that you never breathe out properly and that the chest area is never exercised to its full potential.

If both your hands, one after the other, rise and fall as you breathe, then you are breathing correctly. Air is flowing into the lower part of the lungs first (hand on belly rises) and then spreading into the upper part (hand on chest rises). On breathing out, the air moves from the chest area down into the belly region as it is expelled (hand on chest sinking down marginally earlier than hand on belly).

When you breathe correctly, two processes happen simultaneously as you inhale – your ribcage expands and your diaphragm presses down. This creates increased space in the trunk of your body, permitting the lungs to expand. This process is reversed during exhalation – the ribcage contracts again and the diaphragm moves up so that the lungs deflate and air is expelled. Choose one of the following exercises depending on whether you need to improve your lower or your upper lung activity.

Increasing lower lung activity (belly area)

- Lie down comfortably, loosen tight clothing and put one hand on your belly above your navel.
- Tighten up your stomach and belly muscles so that they tuck in.
- Relax your belly muscles again and feel the difference between tension and relaxation in this area.
- Repeat five times to heighten your awareness of your belly area.
- Rest for a moment and allow your breathing to go whichever way it wants to go. It does not matter whether you breathe quickly or slowly, regularly or irregularly. Now continue as follows:
- Inhale in such a way that the hand on your belly is pushed upwards.
- Breathe out through your mouth, making a long 'HAAAA' sound as you do so. Notice how your belly area deflates and how this makes your hand go down again.
- Repeat this exercise ten times.

Increasing upper lung activity (chest area)

- Lie down comfortably, loosen tight clothing and spread both arms, fully extended, on the floor so that your body forms a cross, your arms making the horizontal line to the vertical line of the rest of your body. Notice how opening your arms out like this creates more space in your chest cavity.
- Now fold your arms tightly over your chest, as if hugging yourself. Notice how this constricts the space your chest has available.
- Repeat this exercise five times.

Take a break for a few minutes, then continue as follows:

- Repeat the exercise, but this time breathe in as you open your arms out and breathe out as you fold them over your chest.
- Repeat this exercise ten times.

Use any lull in activity during the day to take in a few deep breaths through your chest. Only when you can do the first two exercises easily should you go on to the third exercise, which is the same for both groups.

This exercise can be done lying down, sitting up or standing.

Co-ordinating upper and lower lung activity

- Breathe in through your belly area, then let the air fill the chest cavity as well. Do this as smoothly as possible – imagine a wave spreading from the bottom of your lungs to the top.
- Practise this until you can do it effortlessly. In the meantime don't worry about your out-breaths.
- Now co-ordinate your in-breath and your out-breath. Breathe in correctly and allow the air to escape from the top of your lungs first before the belly area 'deflates'.
- Practise this until you can do it smoothly.
- Practise correct breathing three times a day for at least two weeks so that this new, better habit can become more firmly established.

The reason why it makes sense to work on your breathing is two-fold – correct breathing can prevent you from getting stressed in the first place, and it can also help you regain control more quickly once you are stressed.

Giving your body time off

As stress is linked to such a formidable number of physical reactions, it makes sense to help your body regain its balance during and after any stressful period. Although bodily stress reactions are aroused within a split second, they need a much longer time to fade away again. This is where conscious support and assistance can speed up the recovery process.

The following suggestions and exercises will help you to relax and unwind. You will find the exercises particularly valuable if you have sleeping problems.

Allowing yourself to rest

Once you have finished one chunk of work, take a break of five to ten minutes. Here are some suggestions:

- Have a bite to eat. Do this sitting down, and have the food on a plate, even if you are only having three biscuits and an apple.
- If at all possible, remove yourself from your working environment for a moment. Go outside, do a breathing exercise, or walk around the block. A change of scenery, combined with gentle physical exercise, allows the body's stress responses to simmer down.

- Withdraw to somewhere quiet for a moment. Close your eyes for a few moments and allow your body to rest.
- If you are working from home, put on a favourite piece of music. It does not have to be slow or quiet, so long as it relaxes you. Sit or lie down with your eyes closed and listen for a little while. Notice how your body begins to unwind.

In addition to the short breaks suggested above, here are some more comprehensive ways of helping your body to relax:

Giving your back a treat
- Lie down on the floor or on a firm bed; loosen any tight clothing.
- Support your head with a cushion or a rolled up towel.
- Pull your knees up so that your feet are flat on the floor (or bed), hip-width apart, your knees pointing towards the ceiling.
- Let your hands rest on your hips, arms flat on the floor or bed.
- Feel the lower part of your back making contact with the floor or bed.
- Close your eyes and remain in this position as you (slowly) count to 20.
- Now bring your knees up to your chest and hug your legs in towards you. Keep your eyes closed and hold this position to the count of 20.

Feel how your lower back pushes even further into the floor or bed beneath you.
- Go back to the original position and repeat the entire process twice more.

This exercise relaxes your back because lying down relieves the pressure put on the intervertebral discs by gravity. This pressure shortens the back muscles so that fluid is squeezed out from between the discs. By lying down, you take pressure off your back and allow these muscles to relax. As your lower back sinks down onto the floor or bed, the spine lengthens and allows fluid to re-enter the centre of the discs, restoring the cushioning effect of the fluid on the discs.

Loosening muscles
- Lie down on the floor or on a firm bed; loosen tight clothing.
- Support your head with a small cushion. Allow your legs and arms to lie loosely stretched out, arms next to your body. If you suffer from lower back problems, put a thickly rolled up blanket under the back of your knees.
- Close your eyes and tense your feet and lower legs. Hold the tension to the slow count of five. Now release the tension again, repeating in your mind the words, 'Heavy and heavier, sinking deeper' and, if you

can, imagine the muscles in your feet and calves relaxing down into the floor or mattress.

- Take a deep breath in through your nose, hold it for a moment and then exhale slowly through your mouth, making a 'HAAAA' sound as you do so.
- Give yourself a moment to feel the relaxation in your feet and lower legs.
- Now continue with your thighs and buttocks. Tense them up tightly to the slow count of five, then release the tension again, thinking, 'Heavy and heavier, sinking deeper' repeatedly as you let go. Visualize the tension drifting away.
- Take a deep breath again, hold it and release it as before. Feel the relaxation in your feet, legs and buttocks.
- Continue in the same manner for your belly area, your chest, hands, arms and shoulders together, and finally your face (grit your teeth and frown).
- Remain calmly resting on the floor or bed for a while afterwards. You may even drift off to sleep for a moment or two, so if you have other things to do later set your alarm clock before you begin this exercise.

This exercise is highly relaxing because it systematically releases all the tension in your body, and this will also help you sleep better.

Taking a mental holiday

To relax the body is one thing; to relax the mind is quite another and poses its own challenges. Whereas the body reacts quite readily to mechanical exercises like tensing and relaxing, the mind is much less easy to control.

Controlling your mind takes know-how and quite a bit of practice, and some people are better at it than others. In times of stress,

reining in your mind's negative meanderings is crucial, and the best way of doing so is through mental images, also known as visualization. You do not have to be creative or have any particular psychic powers to visualize successfully; all you need is an everyday ability to daydream. This happens naturally when you are looking forward to your next holiday and you can already see yourself in your mind's eye sitting on the beach or on the terrace of your hotel, sipping a drink.

Learning to use visualization for stress control is just as straightforward. You can test your ability to visualize with the following exercise.

Making pictures in your mind

With your eyes closed, imagine

- a house
- a garden
- a street

Take your time. Look at each image carefully. What sort of house are you thinking of? A country or a town house? Modern or old-fashioned? Is your garden well-kept or neglected? What sort of plants are in it? What sort of houses are in your street? Are there any shops?

Once you have spent a little time exploring each image, you should be able to describe it to someone else.

When you go through this exercise you will notice that visualizing is not quite the same thing as seeing with your eyes open. Whereas you get a sharp, focused picture that remains steady when your eyes are open, mental images tend to be much more fluid, more like *ideas* of what something looks like rather than an unchanging reproduction of reality.

In order to achieve mental relaxation during stressful periods, use either of the following two exercises during any breaks you are able to take. The exercises also lend themselves to being done directly after you have completed loosening your muscles as described on page 52.

Accessing past relaxation

Even though you are stressed at the moment, there will have been times when you have been very relaxed. This could have been on your last holiday or when you last visited good friends. You may even have memories of childhood when you happily played outdoors, feeling relaxed and safe.

- Settle down in a chair or lie down. Close your eyes and allow your mind to wander back to the time when you had peace of mind.
- Remember in as much detail as possible. If your relaxing memory is of a past holiday, recall the location, the scenery, the people and the particular occasion when you felt so calm and comfortable.
- Remain in the memory as long as you can. Dwell on it, enjoy it and draw it out.

- One way of prolonging the exercise is by seeking out other memories that are of a similar nature, other times when you felt safe and relaxed and happy with life, and link them with the first memory that came to your mind.

The more details you can collect, the more your mind becomes focused on the task and the more you become immersed in the process of remembering. This will automatically result in a deepening of your physical relaxation as well as a lifting of your mood.

Creating a relaxing image

You may be momentarily unable to access any relevant memories, or perhaps the last relaxing episode in your life occurred so long ago that you cannot remember it in enough detail to make it sufficiently powerful to relax you now.

If this is the case, you can simply invent a relaxing scenario.

- Before you get started, choose from one of the following words the one that you associate most with the notion of relaxation: calmness, peace, tranquillity, serenity, quiet, harmony or stillness.
- Sit or lie down comfortably and close your eyes.
- Repeat your chosen word in your mind. Do so with feeling. Do this slowly, and say the word over and over again until an image begins to emerge that fits the meaning of your word. This may be a real-life scenario such as of walking through beautiful countryside, or it may be a fantasy image such as of drifting along with the clouds in the sky, high above the hustle and bustle of the world.
- Embroider your scenario as much as you can in order to prolong the process of staying with your relaxing image.
- Involve all your senses in your image – sight, sound, touch and smell. The more detailed the image, the better its relaxing effect on your body and mind.

You can change scenarios if you wish, or you can stick to the same one every time you want to relax mentally. Some people have a favourite scene that they know will relax them; others need to alternate between several lest they get bored. Whatever works for you is right.

Sleeping better

How well you sleep will greatly depend on the state of mind you are in before you go to bed. Anyone who worries a lot knows how difficult it can be to drop off to sleep while your mind is still racing with unsettling thoughts.

A good night's sleep is a valuable antidote to stress and the most effective way to rest body and mind. Also, the process of dreaming allows your subconscious mind to deal with the day's events and to work through them, which is vital for maintaining mental health. Sleep, however, is often elusive when you need it most.

Sleeping tablets may appear to be the solution, and they can be helpful in the short term, but they are certainly *not* advisable for long-term use. Sleeping tablets can leave you feeling drowsy right through the next day. And unless you are taking herbal sleeping pills, there is also a chance that you may become addicted to the tablets, either physically or psychologically. Then when you finally do decide to stop taking them (always gradually, and always under a doctor's supervision), you may find your insomnia returns worse than ever.

You are better off using some very effective alternatives to tablets which will help you re-establish a good sleeping pattern without any negative side-effects. The exercises that follow will enable you to stop worrying and prepare your body and mind for sleep. These techniques work best if they are preceded by a breathing and relaxation exercise as described on pages 45 and 52.

Making a mental list

You will be familiar with the old remedy of counting sheep to induce sleep. This works well for some, but the disadvantage is that it leaves your mind with too much room for manoeuvre, even though the monotony of watching sheep hop over a fence does have a soporific effect. However, when you are worried about something, day-problems tend to intrude on your sheep-counting and disrupt it a little too easily. Try one of the following alternatives:

- Make a mental list of all the furniture in your house and/or office. If you are still awake after this, continue by making an inventory of the furniture in your parents' house and the homes of your friends and other family members.
- Make a mental list of all the lights and light fittings in your home, in your office, in your parents' home and your friends' homes.

These exercises require some focused attention together with some neutral visualization of locations, and this creates a very effective distraction from everyday worries.

Create a relaxing blank

When you worry about something at night, you tend to go over the same scenarios again and again, or lose yourself in details about how things could go wrong. This results in a perpetual flow of unsettling thoughts that feed on each other. To bring this vicious circle to a halt, try the following technique:

• List your worries in a matter of fact way in your mind. Formulate each worry concisely, then say to yourself 'next!' and go on to the next worrying thought.

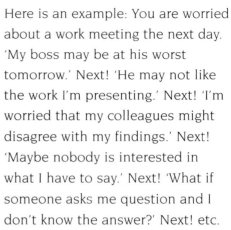

Here is an example: You are worried about a work meeting the next day. 'My boss may be at his worst tomorrow.' Next! 'He may not like the work I'm presenting.' Next! 'I'm worried that my colleagues might disagree with my findings.' Next! 'Maybe nobody is interested in what I have to say.' Next! 'What if someone asks me question and I don't know the answer?' Next! etc.

You will be surprised how quickly you come to a point where you cannot think of another worry. This is when you experience a very pleasant blankness in your mind, and this is often when you automatically slip into sleep. If you find yourself going back to worrying after the blank, just repeat the exercise.

Preparing for sleep

As already mentioned, you will find it very helpful to do one of the breathing exercises or muscle-relaxation (*see pages* 45 *and* 52) to prepare your body for sleep.

Here are a few further tips that will make it easier to unwind:

- Avoid vigorous exercise directly before bedtime. Leave at least two hours between aerobic exercise and going to bed.
- Gently stretching your limbs and holding the stretches for one to two minutes helps the relaxation process.
- Sleep in a cool bedroom, but make sure you are comfortably warm in bed.
- Leave at least an hour before you go to bed after your evening meal, but do not go to bed hungry as the hunger pangs will keep you awake.
- Listening to the radio or to taped novels (not TV!) as you lie in bed with your eyes closed is a very effective way of falling asleep.
- Have a warm (not hot) bath last thing at night.
- Have a warm herbal tea half an hour before bedtime. Chamomile, valerian or vervain are particularly relaxing.
- Avoid alcohol, caffeine and nicotine, if not altogether then at least for five hours or so before you go to bed.
- Avoid working in bed or discussing domestic or work problems in bed. Treat your bed as your sanctuary, where work issues have no place.

- Establish a reasonably steady bedtime routine, including a certain time when you go to bed and when you get up.

Finally, make sure you go to sleep on a positive note:

- Instead of lying in bed reminding yourself of things you could have done or said differently, think of three good things that have happened during the day, no matter how minor. This way you are more likely to go into a deep, satisfying sleep and awake the next day feeling positive.

Accentuate the positive

If you spend a lot of time thinking about something, it takes on its own reality. Persistent worrying about an upcoming exam, for example, will make you physically tense and diminish your ability to concentrate, so that consequently you will do less well than if you had not got so worked up about it.

Normally we are not aware of what we are thinking throughout the day; we tend not to listen to our thoughts while we are thinking them. However, we are aware of how we *feel* and *react* as a result of our thoughts. Thinking about something unpleasant, for example, usually results in accelerated heartbeat, anxious breathing and general physical tension. And as you have already seen in your mental holiday exercise (*page* 54), dwelling on pleasant and relaxing thoughts and images has exactly the opposite effect – muscles relax, the mind unwinds, and this brings with it a sense of peace and well-being.

It is important to pay attention to the quality of your thoughts because they determine how you feel during the day, how well you perform and how well you sleep at night. If you do not get rid of negative thoughts straight away, they can easily begin to fester and grow out of all proportion. You can virtually think yourself into stress.

Acquiring a positive outlook

So how do you get from negative to positive? Is it all a matter of putting on rose-tinted spectacles and pretending everything is fine when, in reality, it is not? No. Positive thinking and an optimistic outlook have nothing to do with walking around with your head in the clouds. Rather, you must work at 'shifting the balance'.

What positive thinking does is to get you into the right frame of mind to demonstrate your skills to their best advantage while you stay calm and focused. This relaxed attitude is also ideal should anything unexpected happen. When you are relaxed you are more likely to deal with problems constructively. So if you have had a firm belief up until now that every silver lining has a cloud, you can significantly reduce your stress levels by acquiring a positive outlook.

Liking yourself

A fundamental prerequisite for viewing the world positively is to feel good about yourself. This doesn't mean you have to consider yourself perfect, but you should at least look upon yourself as good and acceptable. Check how you feel about yourself with the following test.

Test

Sit down, make yourself comfortable and think about yourself.
- What is your immediate emotional reaction? Do you feel comfortable or uncomfortable thinking about yourself?

If you feel calm and relaxed while thinking about yourself, go on to page 72. If thinking in this way makes you feel unsettled because you immediately focus on all your shortcomings, then take some time to do the following exercise.

Shifting the focus

Take a sheet of paper and write down everything you like about yourself. Do not stop until you have put at least three things down; the more the better.

If you find this exercise difficult, think about it from a slightly different angle. How would good friends of yours describe your positive qualities?

Once you have written several of your good points down, sit back and consider how you would feel if you were introduced to someone at a party who had all these positive character traits. Chances are that you would like that person, wouldn't you? So if you have these positive characteristics, you cannot be as bad as you might sometimes feel you are!

Carry your piece of paper with you for a week and look at it once a day to remind you that you are a good and worthwhile person. Spend time dwelling on your accomplishments rather than on your short-comings for a change. Do this first thing in the morning to get the day off to a good start. Once you feel more comfortable about yourself, it is time to tackle the issues that cause you stress.

Using affirmations

An affirmation is a positive phrase that you use repeatedly to feel more optimistic and to put yourself into a frame of mind that allows you to work, act and think more efficiently. The frequent use of affirmations impresses a new and more optimistic 'memory trace' onto your subconscious mind, so that after some practice you find yourself thinking more positively automatically.

Affirmations are general statements that are designed to have an encouraging and uplifting effect, so they need to be phrased carefully. Constructing an affirmation is not difficult, provided you keep to a few basic rules.

Avoid negative phrasing

If possible, your affirmation should only contain positive words. Words which have to do with fear, doubt or failure should be avoided in order to get the full benefit of the affirmation. Instead of thinking 'I am not afraid of public speaking,' think, 'I am confident/calm/relaxed when I speak in public.' Instead of 'I will not make any mistakes in my exam,' think, 'I am doing well in my exam.'

Use the present tense

If at all possible, avoid using future tense such as 'I will do well when I speak to my boss tomorrow.' Instead, say to yourself 'I am calm and relaxed when I speak to my boss.' Your subconscious mind takes things literally, so if you talk of something occurring in the future, your subconscious mind will wait and wait – but you want to feel calm *now*, so that you can approach the event with confidence and perform well when it actually takes place.

Use affirmations regularly

Negative thoughts are usually well established by the time you get around to changing them to positive ones. This means that you might initially notice how the negative thoughts keep coming back into your mind when you are 'not looking'. Old habits die hard, and you will have to persist in replacing negative for positive every time you catch yourself. Be patient; the negative thoughts will gradually become less powerful and will eventually vanish completely.

Positive affirmations for the start of the day

- I look forward to a happy day.

- I look forward to all the good things that are just around the corner.

- I have everything it takes to make this a good day.

- I look forward to this new day with confidence.

Positive affirmations when you are in a difficult situation

- I can do this; I can solve this.

- I am calm, centred and strong.

- As I master this experience, I am getting stronger.

- I am doing my best, and my best is very good indeed.

De-stress your life

Diet

Most people who are under stress eat all the wrong foods. Typical stress-meals include chocolate, snack bars and hamburgers and chips - and not a vegetable or piece of fruit in sight! There is nothing wrong with the occasional bar of chocolate, but when you are stressed you are not doing your body a favour by giving it food that has been processed to death offering nothing by way of fibre, vitamins or minerals but instead leaving you with excessive carbohydrates which produce acids in the body through fermentation.

The foods that turn most readily into energy are those which are left closest to their original state, such as fresh fruit and raw or only slightly cooked vegetables. If you need something sweet when you feel stressed, go for sun-dried fruit. The less energy the body needs to spend digesting food, the more energy is left to help you deal with the stressful situation.

Do's and don'ts

- Sit down when you are eating.
- While you eat, do not do anything else at the same time.
- Chew properly. This helps produce enzymes in the saliva which break down food.
- Do not skip breakfast. Having some food in your stomach first thing improves concentration.

Besides eating sensibly, you can also support your body by supplying it with extra vitamins and minerals. Especially useful are vitamins A, C and E, also known as antioxidants, which help combat free radicals in

the body that can destabilize healthy cells. If you are of a nervous disposition, you will find magnesium very helpful as a supplement. Ideally, take it together with the same amount of calcium. Magnesium has a soothing effect on the nerves and helps you relax better.

Drinking

Seventy-five per cent of the human body consists of water, and 72 per cent of our blood is made up of water. It is the water in the blood that carries nourishment to the cells and helps rid the body of toxins by flushing through the kidneys regularly. It is recommended that you drink between six and eight glasses of water each day to enable your body to function properly. This water should be filtered or bottled; try not to drink tap water too much. Tea and coffee, including decaffeinated coffee, are no substitutes for water! Caffeine dehydrates the body and hypes you up artificially by increasing your heart rate; it can cause insomnia, trembling, nervousness and muscle tension – all conditions you can do without when you are already stressed.

Alcohol may seem to help you relax, but excessive use of it causes the body to accumulate toxins and eradicates the B vitamins and vitamin C as well as minerals. Alcohol can also cause sleeping problems, impairs immune function and makes you feel depressed, thus adding to the already existing stress burden.

Think before you start working

When you are wound up and afraid that you may not be able to do all the work that needs doing, some people tend to rush into activity and press on throughout the day without stopping. You may think you are saving time, but in reality you are floundering without a plan so that in fact you are *wasting* time.

Any activity can be spread over a period of hours or days; planning what you need to achieve each day is crucial. The easiest way to do so is to start the day by making a list.

TO DO:
- TURN IN RECEIPTS
- PACK FOR N.Y.
- GET CASH
- PICK-UP PLANE TICKET
- INVOICE NAPLES INDUSTRIES
- CALL JODI
- CALL MARSHA RE. COMMISSION
- TAX W-9 FORM
- B-DAY PRESENT BROOKS
- DROP DRY CLEANING
- CELL PHONE BATTERY
- BUSINESS MAP.
- PROPERTY RELEASE FORMS <TOWN TOWER
- DISC & SOFTWARE BOOKS
- SPREAD SHEETS FOR ICON GRAPHICS
- FILM
- TIME CARDS
- STAMPS
- LANNY'S B-DAY FRAME
- NEW LICENSE PLATES
- DOG FOOD FOR MAX & SOCKS
- CHANGE OIL & BRAKE FLUID
- POST OFFICE KEY FROM BETH

- List everything you need to do.
- Mark those items that are urgent.
- Now extract those items from the 'urgent' list which you do not like doing – then do them first to get them out of the way!
- Be prepared to cancel or postpone those items which are not very important if you are running out of time.
- Set a time limit of how late you want to work – and stick to it.
- Take breaks, especially when you feel there is no time for a break. Stopping for a few minutes to relax clears your head and helps you concentrate better.
- Make it a rule to complete one task before you start the next. You may not finish everything, but at least you will have completed most items rather than having made only a half-hearted stab at all of them.

Get a move on – exercise!

When you are under stress your body tenses up and various stress hormones are released into the bloodstream. When you do not move your body – for example if you spend a lot of time sitting at a desk – your limbs stay tense and the adrenalin keeps you hyped up for longer than necessary.

   This is where exercise comes into it, and you will be pleased to learn that exercise in this context does not mean hours of workouts five times a week. You can achieve very good results from even just ten minutes of exercise, provided you do it regularly – that is, every other day at least. Working adrenalin out of your system can be fun and does not have to make you go purple in the face. Here are some simple exercise routines which you can do indoors or (weather permitting) out.

Exercise 1 – cycling

- Lie down on your back on a firm mattress or on a blanket on the floor.
- Support your head by putting a small cushion under it.
- Put your arms flat on the floor next to your body.
- Begin to make cycling movements with your legs in the air, but make sure your whole back remains on the ground.
- Count 'one' for every right-left leg movement you do; continue to the count of 60.

Exercise 2 – stretching

- Stand with your face to a wall.
- Place both hands against the wall, keeping your arms straight.
- Pretend you are trying to push the wall away by keeping your right leg bent, right foot flat on the floor, and the left leg stretched out straight behind the right one, left foot flat on the floor. You should feel a gentle stretch in the back of your left leg. (Should the stretch feel uncomfortable, bring your left leg nearer to the right leg.)
- Hold the stretch to the count of 60 (approximately 1 minute), then change feet so the left leg is in the forward position and the right leg behind. Feel the stretch in your right leg. Hold for 60.
- Throughout, make sure you keep your arms are straight and pushing into the wall.

Exercise 3 – running

- Take your shoes off and stand on your bed. Alternatively, fold up an old blanket several times so it becomes really thick. Should you decide to do this exercise on the floor, make sure you wear firm shoes, ideally trainers, to cushion your joints adequately.
- Run on the spot, counting one for every right-left leg movement. Do the exercise to the count of 120.

Now go through the whole sequence of cycling, stretching and running one more time, then finish off with a last stretching exercise. All this will take you about ten minutes. It gets your muscles loose and increases your heart rate so that the adrenalin gets cleared out of your system and your head is 'de-fogged'. Make sure you drink some water, one or two glasses, afterwards so that toxins and body wastes can be eliminated more easily.

   Swimming a few lengths in a pool – just as many as you can do without feeling uncomfortable – or walking briskly for ten minutes are equally good alternatives.

Developing outside interests

Whether you are an executive of an international company or at home with several small children (the workload is approximately the same in both cases!), make sure there is more to your life than the work you are doing! When you are buzzing with activities and duties day in and day out, it is easy to forget your own needs and interests in the process.

Having at least one hobby or interest that you pursue fairly regularly is a safeguard against becoming overwrought. Even if you love your job, it is therapeutic to engage in activities that have nothing to do with work. Whether you like sketching or playing golf, whether you want to roller skate or fly a kite, make the time to do something special, something that is fun and just for you.

By making space for outside interests in your life it becomes possible to take a step back from your work and put it into a more balanced perspective: often, solutions for problems come to mind much more easily once you have stopped thinking about them for a while. Above all, having outside interests is an excellent way of recharging your batteries and gathering fresh enthusiasm.

Alternative ways to unwind

As we have discussed, there are lots of things you can do to keep stress from developing in the first place and to deal with it effectively. Ideally you will always try and deal with the underlying cause of your stress rather than with its symptoms, but that is not always possible. Sometimes all you can do is to hang on in there and deal with a difficult situation as best you can.

If you find yourself in a situation where stress symptoms have become firmly established, it can be useful to get outside assistance to help you unwind. There are a number of natural therapies which can support your own efforts and help you get relief from stress symptoms more quickly. Here are brief descriptions of some of these therapies, to give you an idea of how they can help with stress.

Aromatherapy
Aromatherapy uses essential oils taken from plants, to be massaged into the skin, inhaled or taken orally. If the oil is to be absorbed via the skin, a good aromatherapist will very carefully clean the skin first and then help the skin absorb the oil by applying hot compresses after the oil has been applied. Another way of encouraging the oil to pass

through the skin is by gently massaging it into the face or back.

Aromatherapy oils can benefit a vast range of physical, emotional and mental symptoms. Oils that help with nervous tension are bergamot, chamomile, geranium, jasmine, marjoram, rose and sandalwood.

Hypnotherapy

Hypnosis is a combination of relaxation and concentration, and as such is very useful in combatting the negative effects of stress. A few sessions of suggestion therapy, together with a good self-hypnosis tape, should be sufficient to teach you how to let go of physical stension so that your body and mind can calm down and recharge.

The relaxing effect of hypnosis is usually brought about by suggestions of soothing mental images which you are encouraged to concentrate on. If your stress problem is more complex, analytical hypnotherapy can help.

Reflexology

Reflexology is guided by the principle that various pressure points on the feet correspond to different organs and glands in the body.

After gently feeling your feet, a reflexologist will apply pressure to various points where a 'block' has been detected under the skin. These blocks indicate that the internal organ which corresponds to that particular pressure point is not functioning to its full capacity. By pressing a particular point, the organ is stimulated. Reflexology has achieved good results in treating, among other conditions, stress states, headaches and constipation.

Shiatsu

Shiatsu massage works with the acupuncture points situated along energy paths in the body (also know as meridians). Depending on which meridians are stimulated, the practitioner can help the client feel toned up or calmed down. Shiatsu is used both prophylactically and for specific conditions.

Pressure is applied with the fingers, and sometimes also with the palms or elbows while the client lies on a padded mat. Shiatsu is also useful as a self-help technique.

Positive thinking

Positive thinking counsellors teach you how to access the subconscious level of your mind and how to implant positive suggestions and affirmations there. They also help you uncover any unhelpful beliefs and attitudes you may have so you can change them to more positive and constructive ones.

The methods used are easy to learn and very effective at reducing physical tension and anxiety, and helping you to boost your self-confidence.

Useful Addresses

To find a qualified practitioner, contact:

Aromatherapy Organisations Council
3 Latymer Close
Braybrooke
Market Harborough
Leics LE16 8LN

The Corporation of Advanced Hypnotherapy
PO Box 70
Southport
Merseyside PR8 3JB

The British Reflexology Association
Monks Orchard
Whitbourne
Worcester WR6 5RB

International Council for Reflexology
4311 Stockton Boulevard
Sacramento
CA 95820
USA

The Shiatsu Society
19 Langside Park
Kilbarchan
Renfrewshire PA10 2EP

To find a qualified positive thinking practitioner, contact:

The Peiffer Foundation
39 Minniedale
Surbiton KT5 8DH